Introducing Drum Kit part 3

by George Double

Published by
Trinity College London Press Ltd
trinitycollege.com

Registered in England
Company no. 09726123

© Copyright 2021 Trinity College London Press Ltd
First impression, April 2021

Unauthorised photocopying is illegal
No part of this publication may be copied or reproduced in any
form or by any means without the prior permission of the publisher.

Cover photo: Tas Kyprianou
Printed in England by Caligraving Ltd

Author's note

This sequel follows directly on from *Introducing Drum Kit – part 2*, exploring all the musical, technical and notational elements required for Grades 3 and 4. Through a series of engaging and practical playalong pieces, exercises and a teacher-student duet, each element is progressively introduced, with handy tips and 'Did you know?' boxes throughout to illustrate and strengthen concepts.

I hope you have fun with all the music that follows. Whether you choose to sit performance exams or just play with your friends or at home for pleasure, the important thing is to enjoy your drumming!

Drum legend

Drum kit notation can vary between different publishers and arrangers. The key below is used throughout this series and is becoming more consistently used.

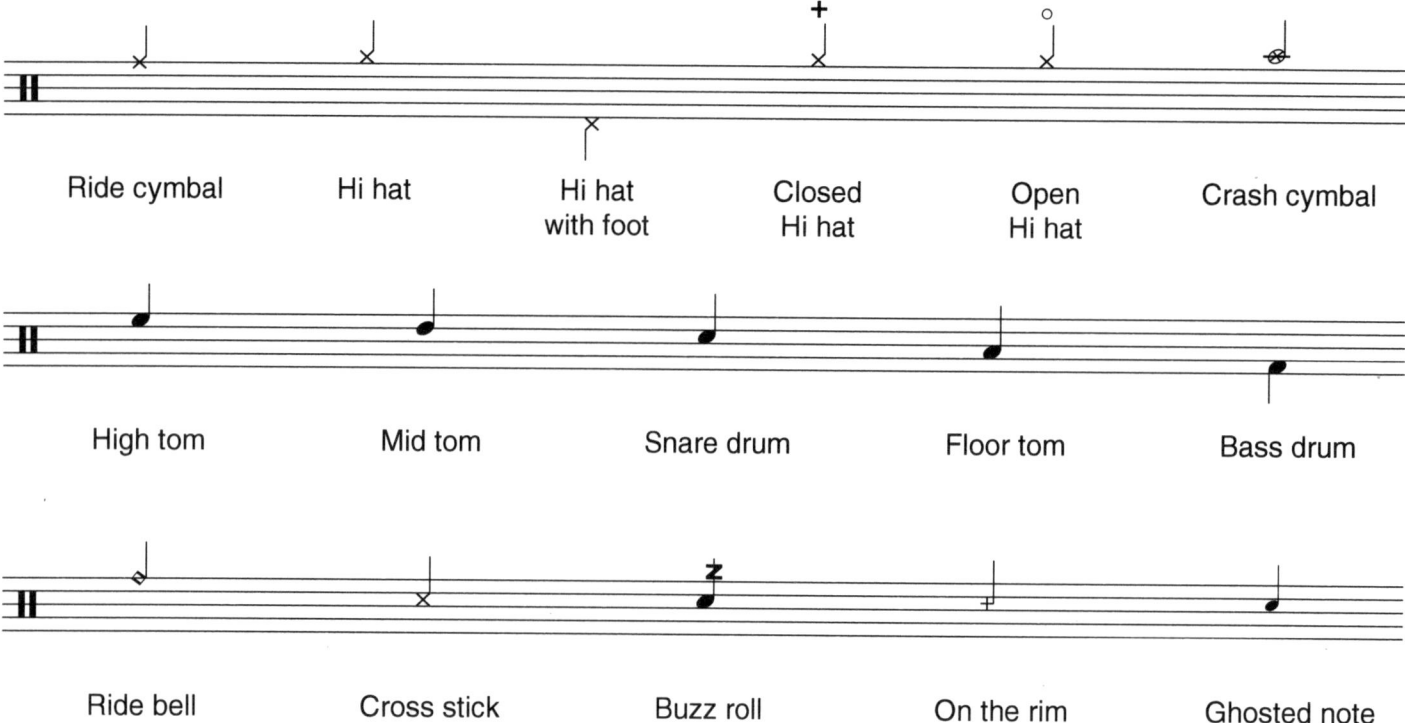

Stage 1

Semiquaver independence & new grooves

As we know, there are four semiquaver beats in a crotchet. We also know that adding a dot to a note increases its value by half. If we break up a crotchet into a dotted quaver and single semiquaver and use it within a straight 8th context, then a number of new groove ideas become available to us. Let's start with a common one, which makes use of left hand independence.

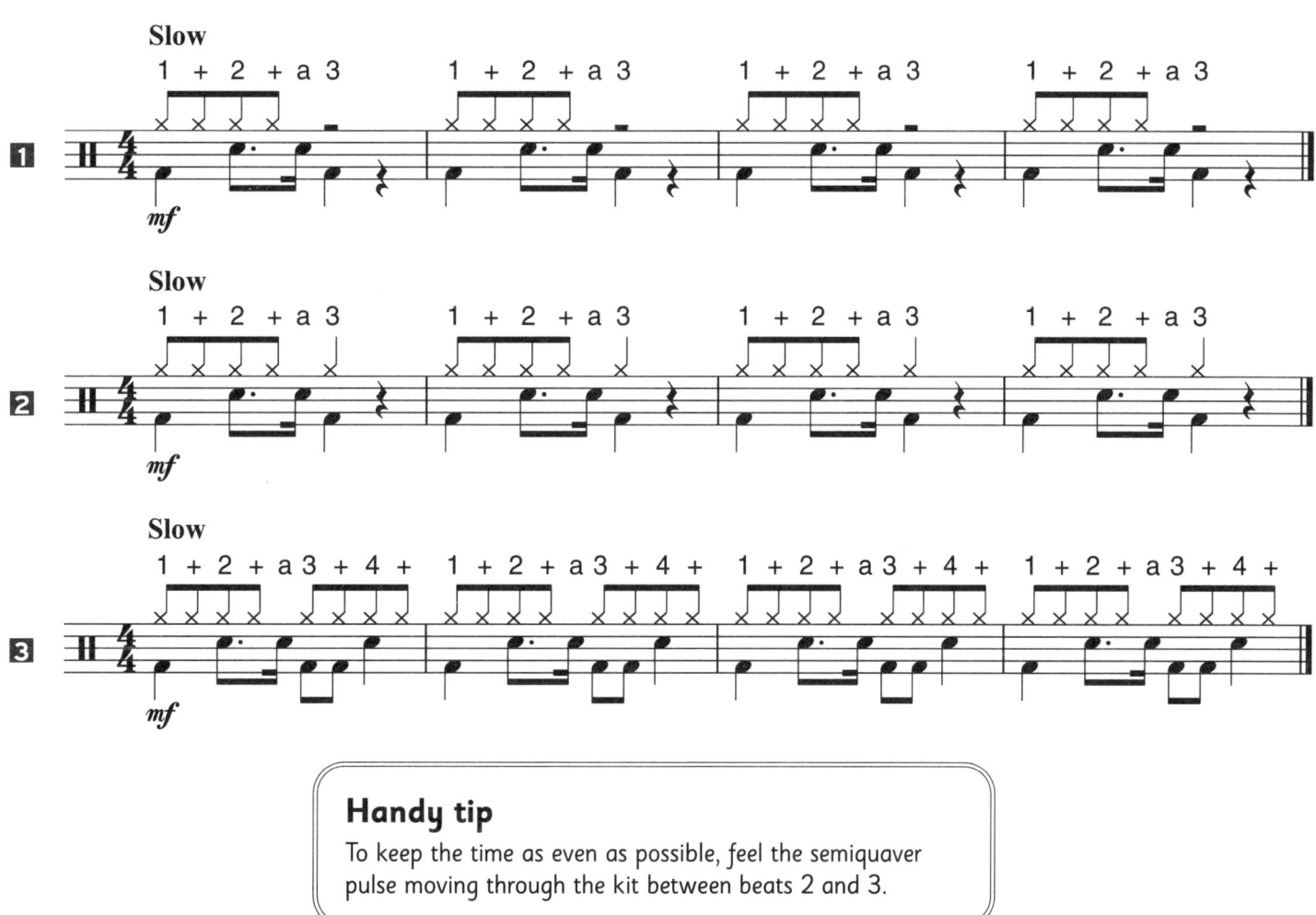

Handy tip
To keep the time as even as possible, feel the semiquaver pulse moving through the kit between beats 2 and 3.

Boogaloo

The groove in the third exercise above is often referred to as a **boogaloo** feel. **Boogaloo** is a type of music which emerged in New York in the 1960s and is a particular mix of rhythm and blues, soul and Latin styles. Early examples of the boogaloo groove include James Brown's 'I Got Money', from 1962, which featured drummer Clayton Fillyau and, later, saxophonist Lou Donaldson's hit, 'Alligator Boogaloo' on Blue Note Records, which featured the great Idris Muhammad (then Leo Morris) on drums. In the same year, 1967, The Staple Singers had a hit with 'For What It's Worth' with a slower, more open version of the groove. Do have a listen to all three tracks.

Since then, Boogaloo feel has taken on it's own identity in the world of kit playing and has been widely used in funk, rock and pop music and has been sampled and often sped up by record producers on dance and drum and bass tracks.

Here are two other groove ideas in this style.

Did you know?

 means to repeat the previous two bars.

Did you know?

Single semiquaver notes joined to quavers have two lines attached to one side of the note stem. One line joins the note to the quaver, the other is shorter, defining the individual note.

Other interesting patterns emerge when we put a snare drum on the second semiquaver or 'e' count of the beat.

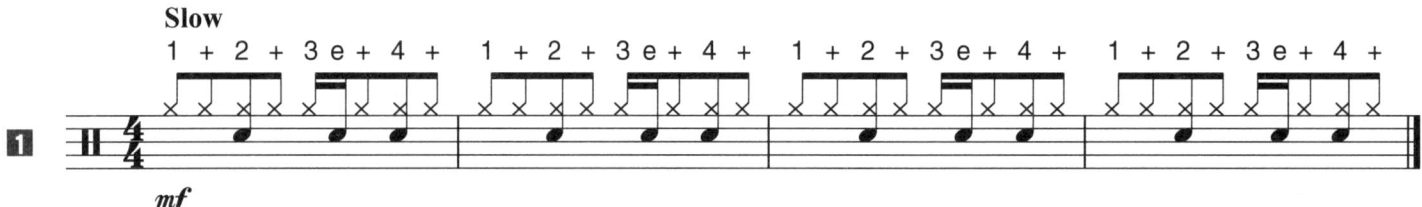

Did you know?

Adding a bass drum often causes the stem direction to change in the notation of this pattern. Stem direction in general is discretionary, and composers and arrangers mostly write drum music in what they hope is the clearest way possible for the player.

Performance piece

Here we put some of these ideas together in a piece in a country-pop style. Note that in the chorus the time signature switches from 4/4 to 2/4 and back again. Get to know how the piece should sound by listening to the demo track. Then you can start to play the piece along with the backing track.

Feel free to use this groove through the verse while getting used to the track, then move to the written pattern when ready.

🎧 Tracks 1a, 1b & 1c

This Old Heart

Country ♩ = 78

Did you know?
Sometimes time signatures change within a piece of music to accommodate phrases or vocal lines of different lengths.

Semiquaver independence on the bass drum

Added semiquaver notes on the bass drum can create all sorts of interesting and fun patterns. If we begin with the same rhythmic idea we used at the beginning of this book (♪. ♪) and put the offbeat semiquaver on the bass drum rather than the snare, we get another classic groove pattern, which has been at the heart of many hit recordings. Here are two preparatory exercises.

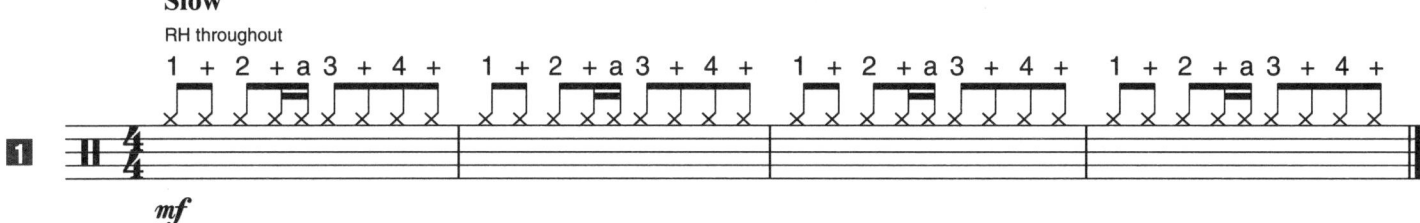

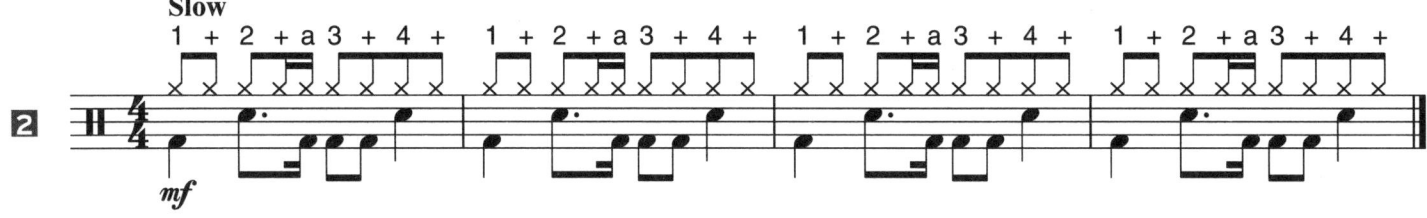

> **Handy tip**
> Keep your right hand as steady and consistent as you can to safely and accurately locate the last semiquaver of beat 2. Fit the bass drum neatly underneath to make the whole thing sit comfortably.

The next exercise may take some time and patient practice in order to achieve fluency. Some people find it helpful to do a half stroke on '(2e+)**a**' on the way down to the hi hat on beat 3. Sometimes it can also be of help to strike out, in the air, to the side of the hi hat at the same point. This prevents any unintended hand motion (caused by the addition of the offbeat bass drum) from causing an unwanted hi hat stroke. In either case, if you stay patient with this groove, it will become more comfortable and fluent.

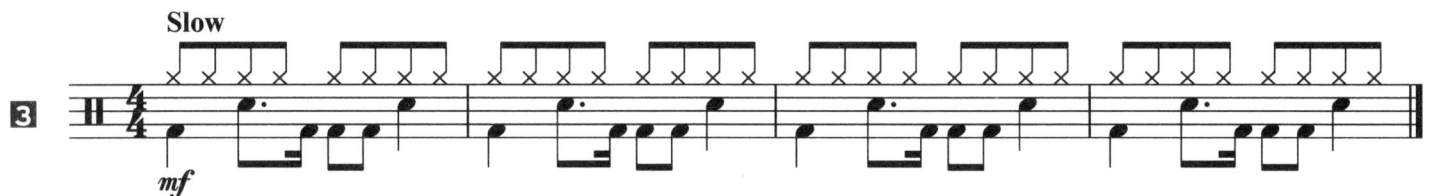

Semiquaver rest

This is a semiquaver (16th note) rest. 𝄿

It represents a quarter of a beat of silence. Here are some exercises to help you get used to playing semiquaver rests.

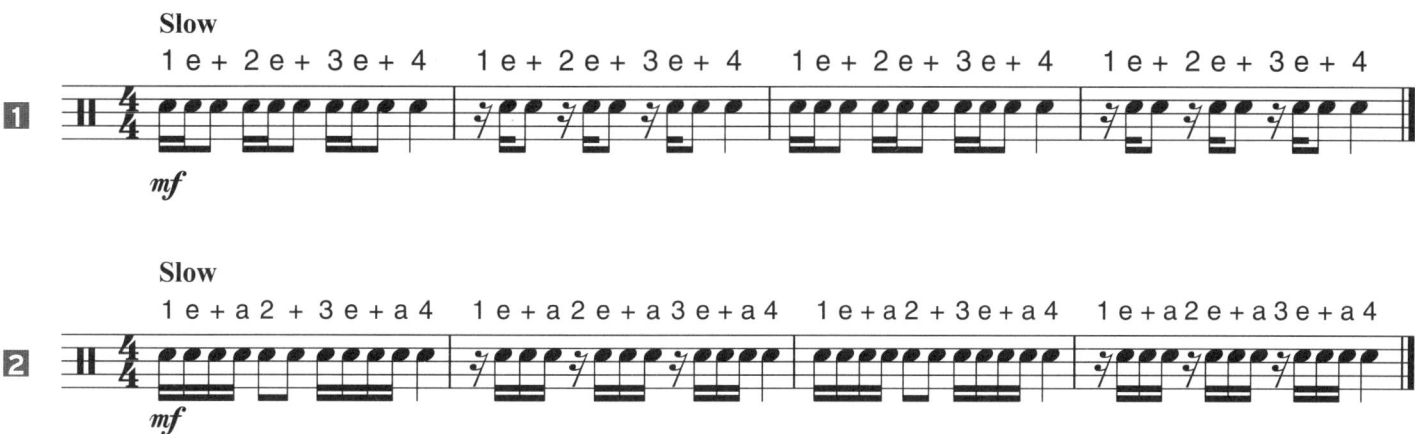

When we group two semiquavers and one quaver together, there are three possible figures that result. We know two of them already:

Here is the third:

Count carefully in the following exercises to ensure the notes are in the right place. Note that the 'and' count appears in brackets above the stave, as the quaver on 'e' lasts for two semiquavers.

Write the count out above the rhythm here. Ask your teacher to check your work if you can.

Subdivision

In music, **subdivision** is the process of breaking up the pulse into smaller parts, with the purpose of understanding and then playing a musical phrase with rhythmic accuracy and confidence. It is a technique which drummers use to develop their timekeeping across all styles of music.

There are many aspects to subdivision, but we will start with a simple idea, which has great relevance to the grooves introduced here and to the rhythmic possibilities that come about with the arrival of the semiquaver rest.

Begin by identifying the shortest note value in a phrase or groove. For our purposes this will be the semiquaver. Count the semiquaver pulse throughout the whole idea and see how the different note values are located in terms of the subdivided count. For example:

Notice there are only two semiquavers in this four bar phrase, but our constant and patient counting of the semiquaver pulse throughout will ensure that these, AND all the other notes, are accurately located, just where they want to be. Also, that our playing will be steady and consistent.

Try using subdivision with the following exercises.

> **Handy tip**
> Use the semiquaver subdivision throughout, not just when playing semiquavers.

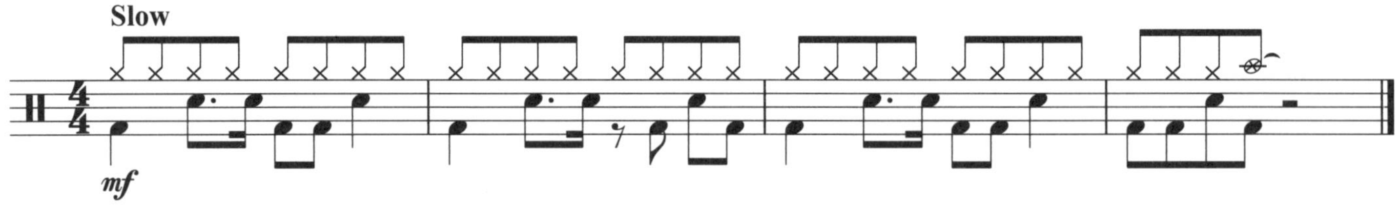

Performance piece

Get to know how the piece should sound by listening to the demo track. Then you can start to play the piece along with the backing track.

🎧 Tracks 2a, 2b & 2c

A Secret

Stage 2

The 16-beat groove

In the 1970s, during the days of disco, a new groove was developed. In its simplest form, drummers played single-stroke semiquavers (16th notes) between hi hat and snare drum, with the snare drum coming on beats 2 and 4, over bass drum on beats 1 and 3. Because of the use of semiquavers, this type of groove is known as **16-beat feel**, in the same way as the use of quavers on hi hat or cymbal is referred to as 8-beat feel or 'straight eighths'. Two good examples of this sort of groove are 'You to Me Are Everything' by The Real Thing, which was a UK no. 1 in 1976, and 'Good Times', a 1979 hit for the band Chic, featuring Tony Thompson on drums.

Let's begin with hi hat and snare drum only.

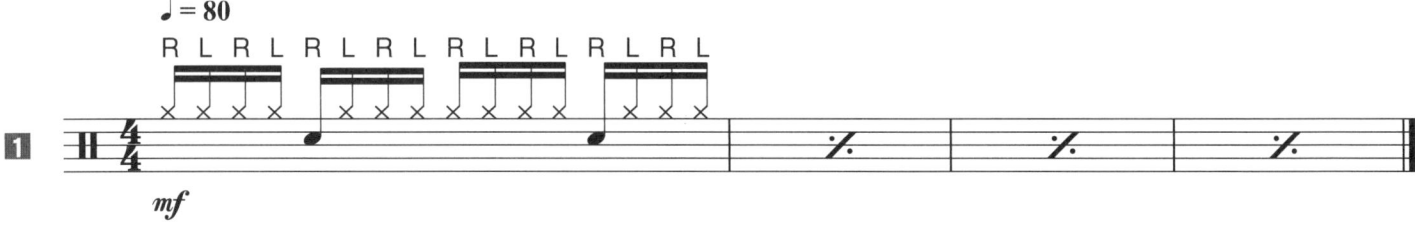

Handy tip

Remaining balanced and in full control of the sound when playing 16-beat patterns can be tricky. Move first from the waist, swivelling the upper body a little towards the hi hat, allowing you to play the 16s from a balanced position. Sitting up straight can allow for a little more room for the snare drum stroke to occur confidently on beats 2 and 4, and some movement in the shoulder can help maintain a purposeful sound as the leading hand moves between the two playing surfaces.

Now we add some bass drum.

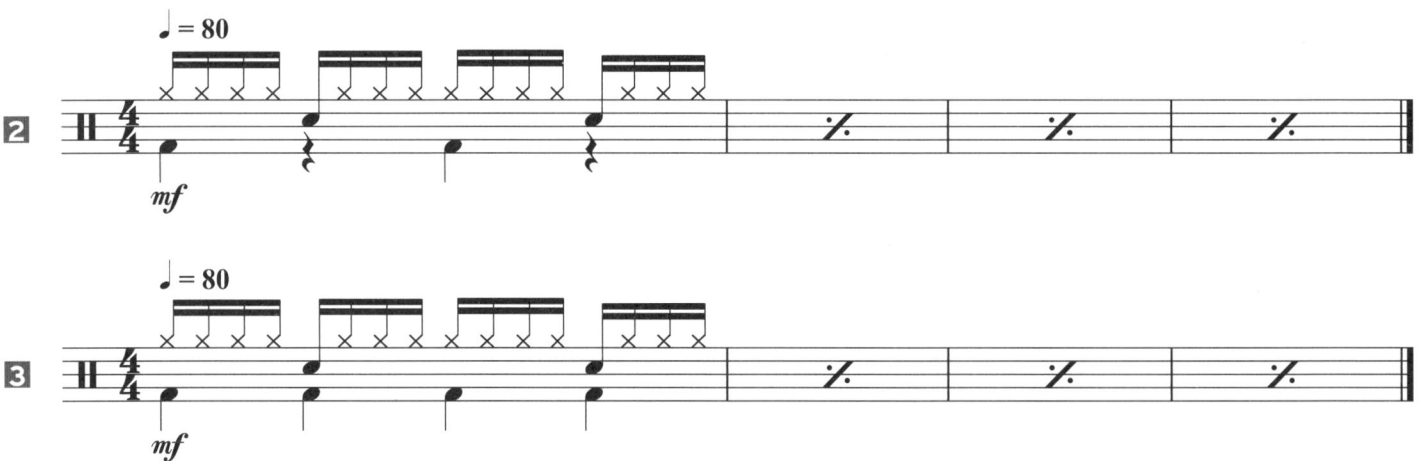

Handy tip

Try these two grooves with either 'You to Me Are Everything' or 'Good Times' or ask your teacher for suggestions of other suitable tracks to play along with for fun. Remember, the stick wants to rebound naturally from the hi hat after each stroke, don't fight it. Keep the grip loose and the stroke flexible enough for the stick and hi hat to do some of the work for you. Allow the rebound to occur and the stick to move freely within the fulcrum, while keeping enough 'snap' in the stroke to maintain a decisive backbeat on the snare.

> **Did you know?**
> The term 'backbeat' refers to the strong accenting of beats 2 and 4 within a bar of $\frac{4}{4}$ time, which of course is at the heart of what we drummers do all the time.

Exercises

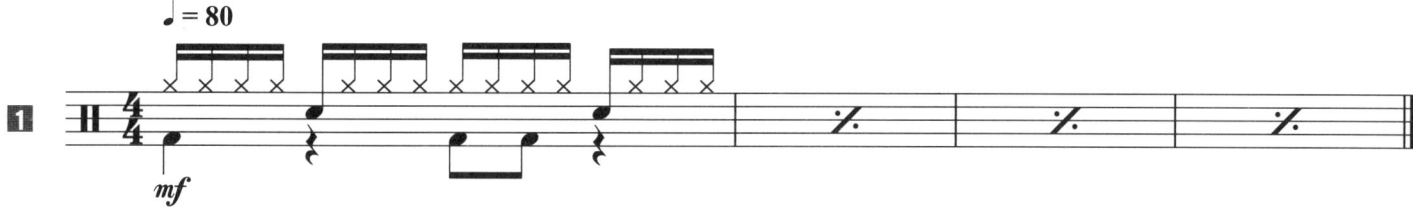

> **Note**
> Sometimes you will encounter 16-beat grooves with bass drum stems going upwards into the hi hat note. This allows you to see clearly on which beat of the bar the bass drum strokes occur.

Performance piece

Get to know how the piece should sound by listening to the demo track. Then you can start to play the piece along with the backing track.

 Tracks 3a, 3b & 3c

No More a Stranger

Disco ♩ = 98

Stage 3

Dynamics

We are aware of dynamic markings and the power of dynamics to create contrast within music. Not only can we create contrast, but we can also build musical tension and release and, most importantly, use dynamics to shape our sound within an ensemble.

Here is a reminder of the terms we already know, and a couple of new ones to add to the list:

pp - *pianissimo* or very soft

p - *piano* or soft

mp - *mezzopiano* or moderately soft

mf - *mezzoforte* or moderately loud

f - *forte* or loud

ff - *fortissimo* or very loud

These terms are not absolute. In other words, *fortissimo* doesn't mean 126.75 decibels precisely. Dynamics are relative, *mf* is louder than *mp* but softer than *f* within the same piece of music and all levels should be suitable for your group and your playing situation. *ff* with a rock band at Wembley Arena is going to be louder than *ff* when accompanying an unamplified choir of young schoolchildren in their end of year show. Always think about your playing within the musical context. Am I playing at the right dynamic level for this tune, with these people, in this venue? Or, when preparing exam performances, does the level of my playing sit correctly with the level of the backing track? Is this sound the right level for this room? And so on.

Subito dynamics

Subito is the Italian word for 'suddenly', or 'immediately'. In music, we can create drama and excitement with sudden changes in dynamic and these are notated as *subito* or *sub.* for short. For example *sub. p* directs a sudden move to *piano* from whatever dynamic came before. Strictly speaking any new dynamic instruction means to change the level directly of course, but *subito* dynamics have the implication that a sudden change is required for a particular effect in the music.

Here is a duet to play with your teacher or with the backing track. Think about your sound throughout your performance to exploit all the dynamic markings for their full effect. If you have a friend who also plays drums, why not try to work out the duet together with one of you playing the teacher's part? The parts are of similar difficulty, and it would make a good concert piece.

Did you know?
The term **Allegro** is a tempo marking, used in classical music, which means quickly and brightly.

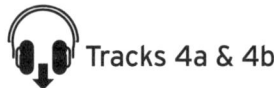 Tracks 4a & 4b

A Pair of Snares

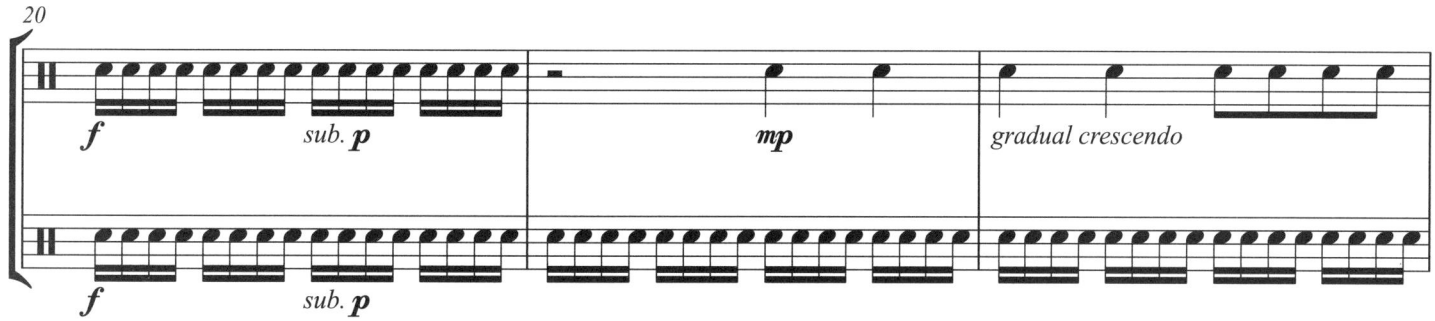
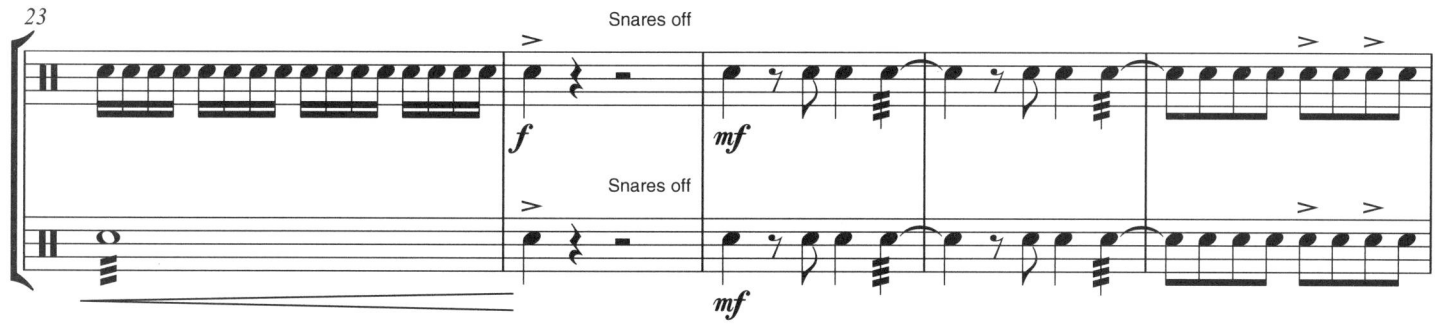

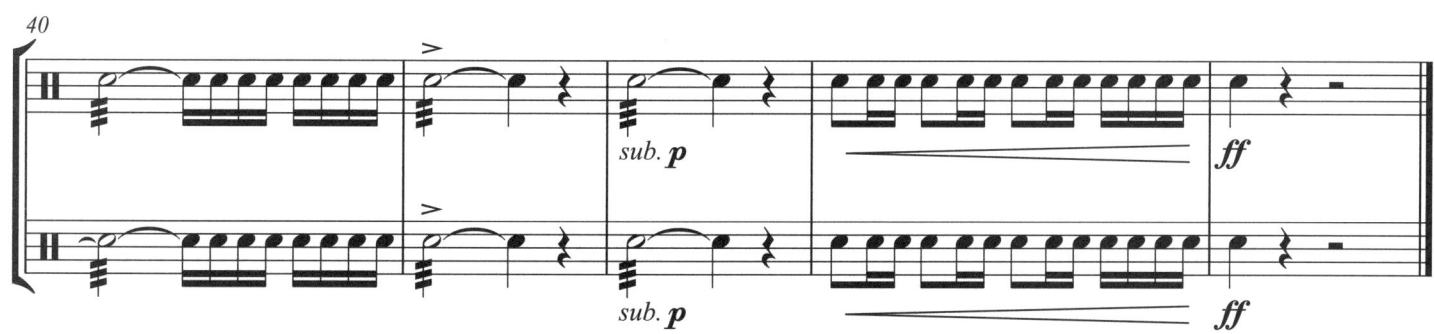

15

Stage 4

Double sticking and new rudiments

Let's look at double sticking. We know that RRLLRRLL means double strokes, or two with each hand, in order. We will now move that idea along to look at **bounced double strokes**, which opens up a whole new world of possibilities.

> **Did you know?**
> Bounced doubles occur when a second stroke is generated from the rebound of the first.

Fluent double sticking isn't easy, and requires very patient practice over time. However, you will get there! Let's start with the most basic form of the double stroke roll. Also known as the 'Mama Dada' roll for the sound it produces.

Play this exercise at various tempos – experiment, repeat, experiment, repeat.

> **Handy tip**
> Play with a broad stroke and throwing motion. Allow the first stroke to rebound and then, using the third, fourth and fifth fingers, snap the stick to produce the second stroke with the same hand. You should aim for a consistent, balanced sound between the first and second strokes and between hands. Play the Mama Dada round and round and round and then round and round again, trying different tempos and on different playing surfaces – drums, practice pad, your leg, the carpet etc – to develop this technique. You will start to experience the FEEL of how bounced double sticking comes about, how the stick moves in your hand, how it works sympathetically with the playing surface and indeed how all three elements – hand, stick and drum – interact with each other to produce the smoothest version of this technique.

In this stage we will look at three new rudiments which use this technique, These are the five-stroke roll, the seven-stroke roll and the nine-stroke roll. Measuring rolls in this way builds our awareness of how rolls work and how they should be constructed at different tempos and for specific durations of musical time.

As a contrast to the multiple bounce or buzz roll, five-stroke, seven-stroke and nine-stroke rolls are made up of double strokes. (Left handed players should reverse the sticking below).

five-stroke roll   RRLLR LLRRL
seven-stroke roll   RRLLRRL LLRRLLR
nine-stroke roll   RRLLRRLLR LLRRLLRRL

> **Did you know?**
> Double stroke rolls are also known as 'open' rolls whereas multiple bounce or buzz rolls are also known as 'closed' rolls.

In *Introducing Drum Kit – part 2*, when learning how to play multiple bounce or 'buzz' rolls, we learned that putting three slashes through a note stem means to play a roll for the duration of that note.

Putting diagonal slashes through a note stem is a type of rhythmic shorthand. The number of slashes across a note stem indicates what type of note should be played for the duration of the written note. For example:

Any note can have slashes added. Here are some more examples:

Quavers already have a line, called a beam, attached to their stems. A slash across the stem acts as an additional beam and will divide that note further into semiquavers.

This is a demisemiquaver or 32nd note. It is a note which lasts for a half a semiquaver or a 32nd of a beat.

A demisemiquaver is half the value of a semiquaver and is very commonly used when playing five-stroke, seven-stroke and nine-stroke rolls. When we see semiquavers with slashed note stems, we generally play demisemiquavers as bounced double strokes.

Though, strictly speaking, three slashes through a note stem could always mean play demisemiquavers, it is very important to remember that, for drummers, three slashes through a note stem is a direction to roll for the duration of that note. Whether we choose to play that roll as buzzes or as rebounded doubles should depend on what is right for the musical situation.

For the purposes of learning about five-stroke, seven-stroke and nine-stroke rolls we will stick to this technical approach when playing the exercises and duets below.

Here are some exercises using slashed note stems and bounced doubles. In all of the following bounced double stroke exercises, feel free to experiment with the order of sticking. Firstly, two exercises to create five-stroke rolls.

For seven-stroke rolls, a practical way in is to use triplet quavers and turn them into bounced double stroke triplet semiquavers.

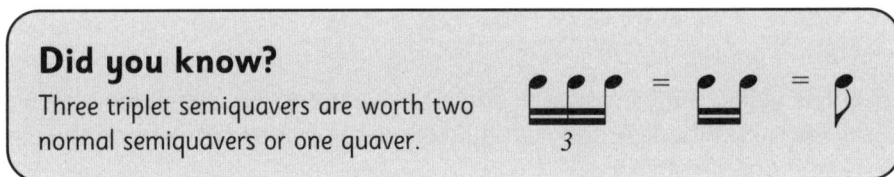

> **Did you know?**
> Three triplet semiquavers are worth two normal semiquavers or one quaver.

We will discuss these notes more fully later in the book. For the following exercises, bounce the individual triplets turning them into double strokes to create the roll, concentrating on the sound and technique. Experiment with playing them at various speeds.

Exercises

18

And now nine-stroke rolls.

The bell of the ride cymbal

The 'bell' of the cymbal is the raised dome-shaped part in the middle. It produces a thick sounding 'ting' sound when struck with the stick. The bell of the ride cymbal, which can often be used in grooves, is notated on the top line of the stave with a diamond notehead.

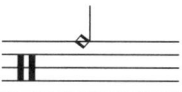

Handy tip
When playing rock or funk grooves, strike the ride bell roughly two to three inches down from the tip of the stick to achieve a rich and well projected sound. In softer contexts, experiment with using the tip of the stick on the bell. Always aim for the most appropriate sound to suit the musical context.

Did you know?
Two to three inches from the tip is where the shoulder of the stick tapers out into the area known as the shaft. Here is a diagram showing you the various regions of the stick and how they are known.

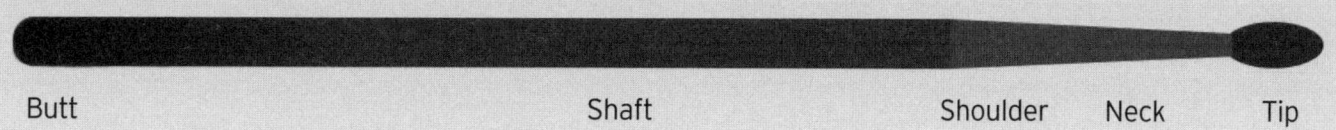

Butt · Shaft · Shoulder · Neck · Tip

Try these exercises using the bell of the ride cymbal.

Performance piece

Get to know how the piece should sound by listening to the demo track. Then you can start to play the piece along with the backing track.

 Tracks 5a, 5b & 5c

All about the Bounce

Handy tip

A four-piece kit set up makes the ride cymbal more accessible to us. For this piece, try removing the mid tom, if you have one, and bring the ride cymbal closer in. That might make the ride bell passage easier to play and should make a consistent bell sound more achievable.

Stage 5

Guide charts and rhythmic markings above the stave

The way in which drum music is presented can vary in different musical situations. Exam pieces are generally very clear and detailed, as you may have seen. Other music you encounter, in bands, musical theatre and elsewhere, may not always be laid out in standard drum notation. 'Guide' charts and lead sheets are forms of sheet music which provide us with information about a piece of music while relying on our knowledge and experience as players to fill in specific musical detail.

> **Did you know?**
> A drum guide or guide chart/part for drums is a very common form of notating the requirements of a piece of music for a drummer, while leaving scope for interpretation and individuality.

Guide charts may contain some standard drum notation for any particular grooves within the piece, and any other detail such as rests and specific rhythmic figures. These directions may also occur as rhythmic markings above the stave (see below). There will be information about tempo, feel, intensity, dynamics and so on and the main body of the chart will often be made up of slash notation, repeat bars and *cont. sim.* passages, giving us the structure, but leaving room for our own interpretation.

> **Note**
> Many of the elements of guide charts will not be new to you – slash notation, *cont. sim.* etc have been covered in this and previous *Introducing Drum Kit* books. However, the addition of rhythmic markings above the stave in particular (see the extract below) lends a greater sense of personal interpretation to a chart hence the overall feel of a 'guide' rather than a stricter, more rigid arrangement containing passages of *cont. sim.* and improvised fills etc.

> **Did you know?**
> Sometimes guide charts will reference a particular piece of music to give you an idea of what kind of groove is required. The basic feel of this arrangement of 'Wayfaring Stranger' takes its influence from the Ramsey Lewis Trio's recording of 'The 'In' Crowd'. Look this recording up and listen to the great feel the band creates, to use as as a starting point. That recording featured Redd Holt on drums.

Groovy '60s feel à la 'In' Crowd (Ramsey Lewis Trio)

♩ = 140

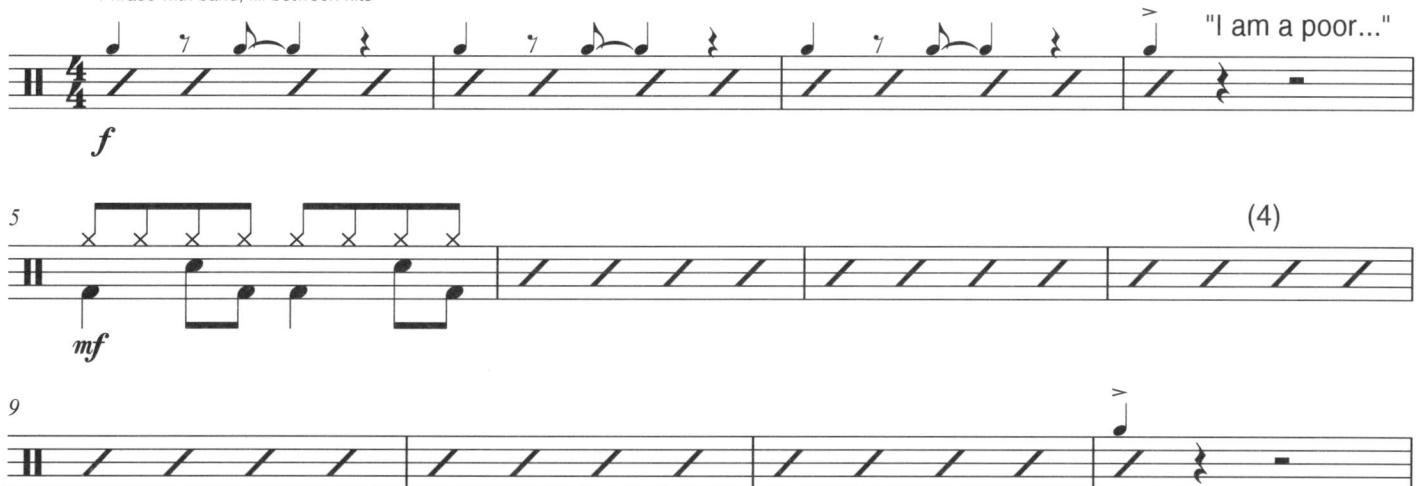

Lead sheets present the harmonic content of the piece, as chord symbols and often but not always, the melody in staff notation. There will also be directions as to time and key signatures, style, tempo and any particular detail that may be required.

Here is an extract from a lead sheet for the song 'Indiana':

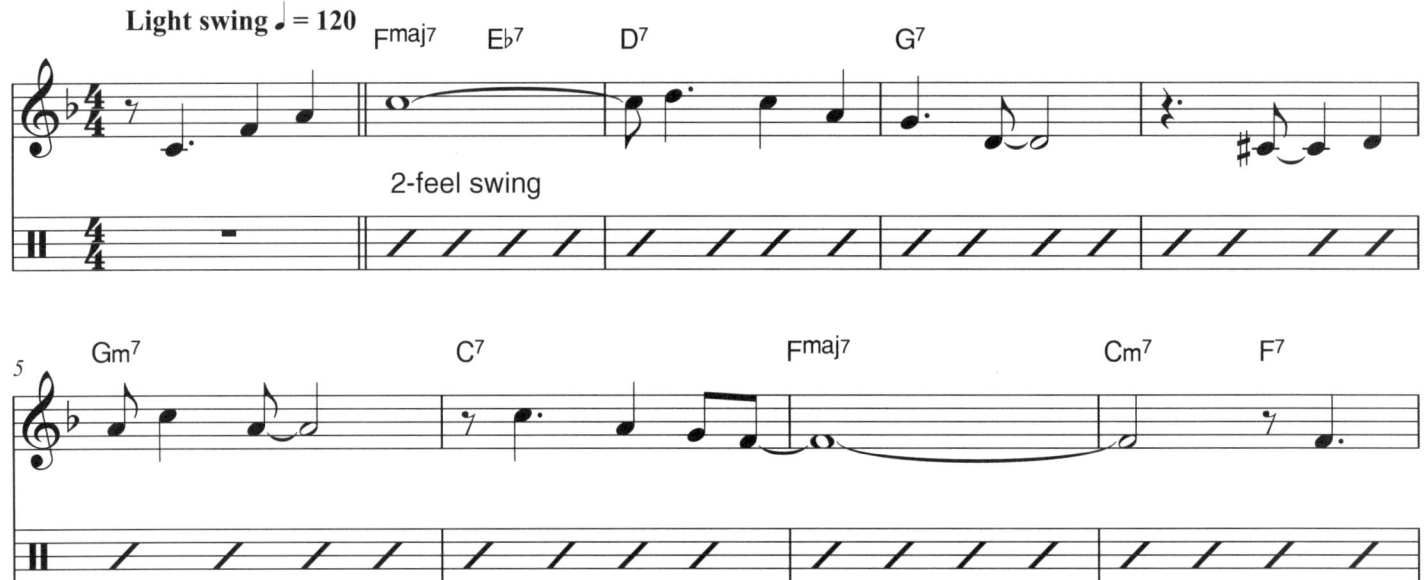

Did you know?
A lead sheet is a guide to how a piece of music should be played and can be used by all instruments, not just drums.

Rhythmic markings above the stave

Guide charts and lead sheets often include rhythmic figures which appear above the stave, usually on the top line where the hi hat is notated. These markings are referred to collectively as **ensemble figures, phrasing marks** or simply **hits.** They direct us to points of rhythmic importance within the piece and instruct us as players to incorporate these rhythmic patterns into our playing.

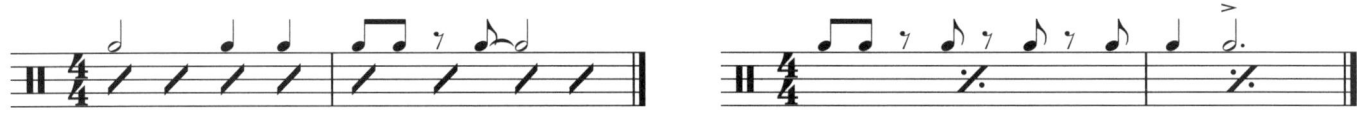

Knowledge of the style, of the musicians around you and awareness of the function of the rhythmic figures within the piece and ensemble sound are key to how best to approach a given figure. There are limitless possibilities for how ensemble marks can be interpreted. Think what is most appropriate in the specific musical situation.

Performance pieces

Here are the full versions of the guide chart and lead sheet we saw earlier. Get to know one version of each piece by listening to the demo tracks. You should feel free to experiment with the figures and notation to see what might work best when playing along to the backing tracks. Appropriate playing for the style and musical suitability should always be at the front of your mind when interpreting the content of these charts.

 Tracks 6a, 6b & 6c

Wayfaring Stranger

Groovy '60s feel à la 'In' Crowd (Ramsey Lewis Trio)

This arrangement of 'Indiana' contains some new text directions.

> ### Did you know?
> **2-feel swing** in 4/4 time directs the bass player to play 2 minims per bar, lending a loping feel to the sound. Drummers often but not always keep time on hi hat in these sections. We are later directed to move to **4-feel swing** (bar 33) where the bass '**walks**' or in other words, plays crotchets. This builds intensity, and drummers will generally move to the ride cymbal here to support the new feel.
>
> There are several '**breaks**' within the arrangement (bars 16, 31-32 and 64). A break suggests a short solo moment for one instrument while the rest of the ensemble stops playing briefly.
>
> The bass and drums are directed to **solo over stops** (bars 49-56 and 57-63). A **stop chorus** in jazz is where the rhythm section play only on the first beat of each bar or a similar variation as in this arrangement, allowing the soloist to fill the rest of the space.
>
> The stops and breaks themselves are marked here as bass drum and snare drum together, as you will often see in this sort of arrangement. Feel free to play them on whatever part/s of the kit that sound best to you however, and listen to the demo to hear one interpretation.

Tracks 7a, 7b & 7c

Indiana

Stage 6

Ghost notes

Ghost or ghosted notes are softer than normal notes. They are most commonly found on the snare, in groove patterns, fitting snugly between the other elements of the groove and weaving an extra layer of texture into the overall sound. They are written with a smaller notehead than normal notes.

Ghosted snare notes can be heard surrounding the snare backbeat on many hit songs. Listen to Bernard Purdie's playing on Steely Dan's 'Babylon Sisters' and David Garibaldi's groove on Tower Of Power's 'Squib Cakes' for exciting and contrasting examples of what can be achieved with ghosting.

> **Handy tip**
> Begin with the snare drum stick in the down position, with the tip roughly an inch from the drum head. Then, simply drop the tip of the stick on to the head of the snare drum for a single stroke and allow the stick to rebound naturally into your grip.

Hear the difference between normal and ghosted crotchets on the snare drum in this exercise.

The boogaloo groove is a very common place to find notes being ghosted. Try this eight bar passage, at a slow tempo, playing the offbeat semiquaver as a ghost note, and hearing the contrast produced between that snare drum note and the notes on two and four.

Performance piece

Here are two contrasting pieces of music that make use of ghost notes.

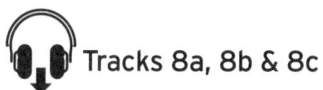 Tracks 8a, 8b & 8c

I'll Be Alright

Performance piece

 Tracks 9a, 9b & 9c

All for Nothing

Stage 7

New rudiments

Grace note rudiments can be extended by the addition of other notes to make new patterns which then become rudiments in their own right. Snare drum rudiments come from a military tradition going back as far as the early 1600s. Although their application on the drum kit in modern music is different to their original purpose, and although some rudiments are more directly suited to kit than others, they do present an excellent framework for technical development and control of sound. They also help build musical vocabulary at the kit and are a starting point for any number of creative ideas.

Here are four new flam-based rudiments.

Handy tip

Practise these individual rudiments with a metronome, starting at a very slow tempo before getting gradually faster, to build confidence and familiarity with the patterns. Make sure the grace notes remain softer than the main notes.

Here are four exercises in which each of these rudiments can be used at the drum kit, either in a fill or as part of a groove pattern.

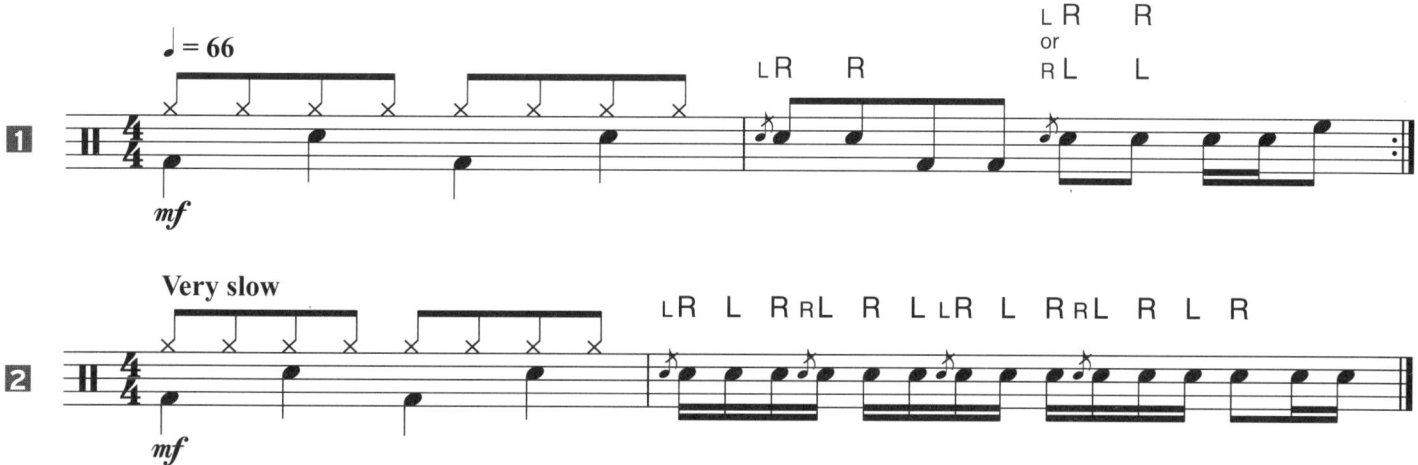

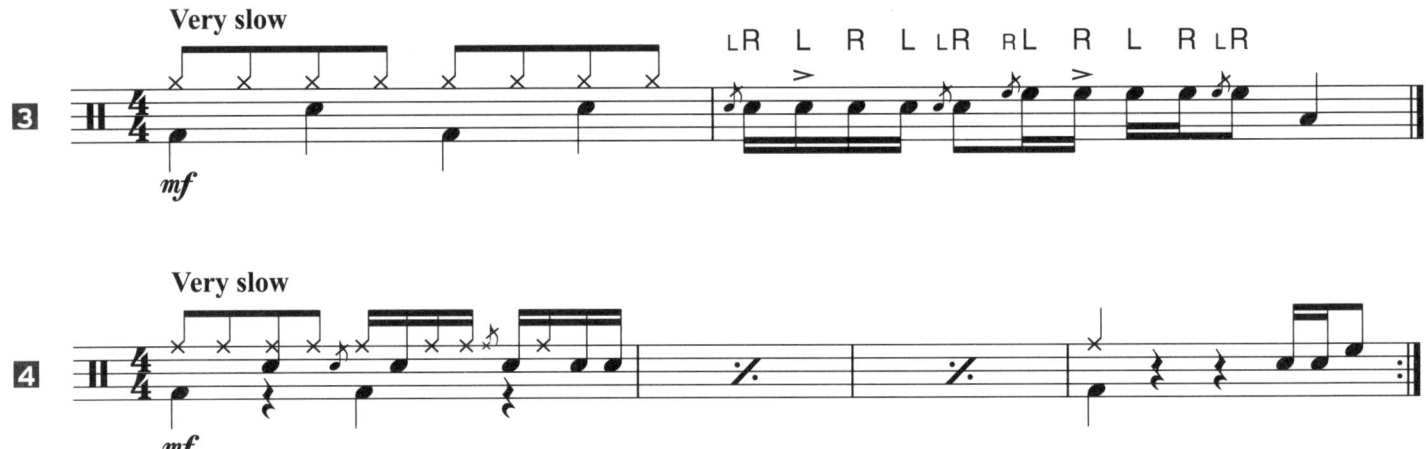

Triplet semiquavers

We learned a little about triplet semiquavers in Stage 4 of this book, when playing seven-stroke rolls.

As we know, three triplet semiquavers are equal to two normal semiquavers or one quaver. A common way of counting triplet semiquavers is to turn the quaver pulse into a triplet count.

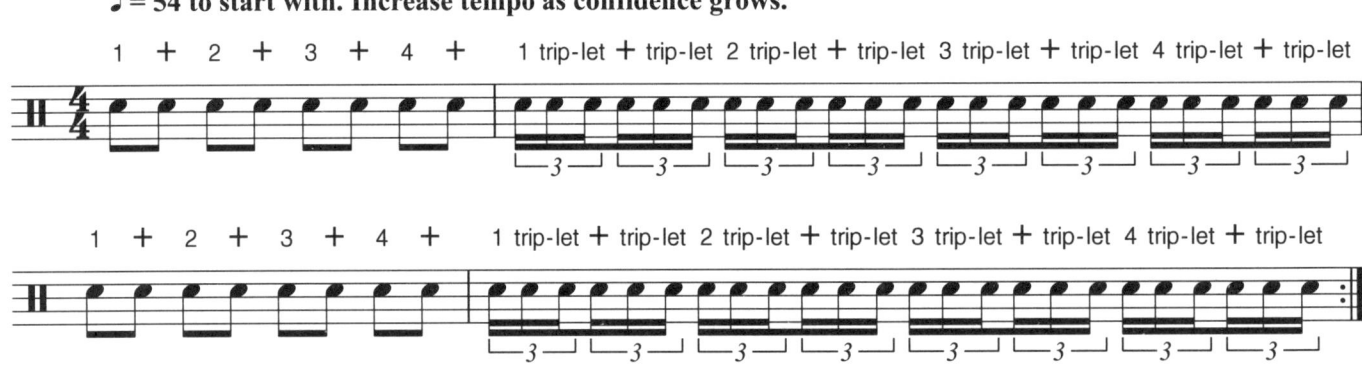

Here are some exercises to help you get used to playing triplet semiquavers.

Sometimes when six triplet semiquavers occur consecutively, they can be put in a group of six, rather than two groups of three.

Did you know?
When triplet semiquavers are grouped in sixes, the notes are also known as **sextuplets**.

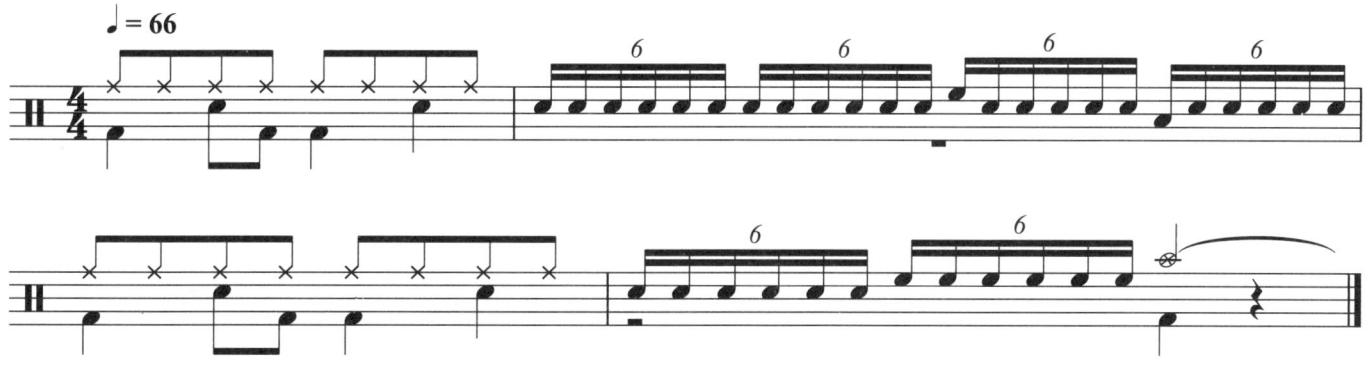

New paradiddle rudiments

Double paradiddles and **paradiddle-diddles** are patterns based on paradiddles and both contain six notes as a combination of single and double strokes.

Double paradiddle

R L R L R R L R L R L L

Paradiddle-diddle

R L R R L L R L R R L L

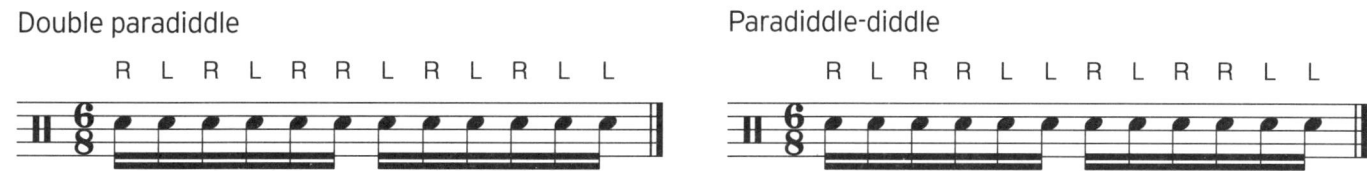

Did you know?
The term 'diddle' in a rudiment directs you to do a double stroke.

Here are some exercises to help you get used to playing double paradiddles and paradiddle-diddles.

Performance piece

Here is an arrangement of the old folk melody 'The Lilting Banshee'. The drum kit part makes use of the six new rudiments we have learned here. Feel free to dip in and out of the written chart and create your own fills when getting used to the patterns as the rudiments are a challenge. Get to know how the piece should sound by listening to the demo track. Then you can start to play the piece along with the backing track.

Tracks 10a, 10b & 10c

The Lilting Banshee

Did you know?

The drums on the demo of this piece are played with rutes rather than standard drumsticks. Rutes are bundles of wooden dowels, bound together. They produce a mellow sound that can be suitable for folk or other acoustic/unamplified music. Rutes are often called 'Hot Rods' too, which is a popular model of this type of beater produced by the Pro Mark company.

Stage 8

Bossa nova

In the 1950s and '60s, a cool, laid-back mix of jazz and Latin American music emerged called **bossa nova**. The term broadly means 'new style' or 'new way'. 'Desafinado' was a big hit for American saxophonist Stan Getz, reaching number 11 in the UK singles charts in 1962 and was taken from the album *Jazz Samba*. 'The Girl from Ipanema', arguably the biggest bossa nova hit, was, like so much of the repertoire, written by Brazilian composer Antonio Carlos Jobim. Have a listen to both of these pieces of music to get an idea of the style.

The bossa nova groove uses a bass drum pattern which is also the rhythm played by the *surdo* drum in a samba band. The cross stick plays a version of a traditional *clave* rhythm, with the last note displaced by a quaver.

Did you know?

The **surdo** drum, is a large, bass toned drum used in samba music. It can be played on a stand or carried with a strap when required. **Clave** in English means 'key'. It is a rhythmic figure used in Latin American music which defines the overall rhythmic character of a piece.

Here are some exercises to build up the bossa nova rhythm.

Handy tip

Play the following exercises slowly and remain aware of the steady quaver pulse in order to locate the cross stick and bass drum notes that come in unexpected places. Do your best to make sure the hands and feet line up neatly together.

Performance piece

Here is an arrangement of the jazz standard 'Indian Summer' in the style of Antonio Carlos Jobim. Get to know how the piece should sound by listening to the demo track. Then you can start to play the piece along with the backing track.

> **Did you know?**
> A jazz 'standard' is a compostion which is widely known and commonly performed by jazz musicians.

> **Did you know?**
> This arrangement makes use of the term 'Head'. The **head** is the term often used for the main melody or theme in jazz tunes.

 Tracks 11a, 11b & 11c

Indian Summer

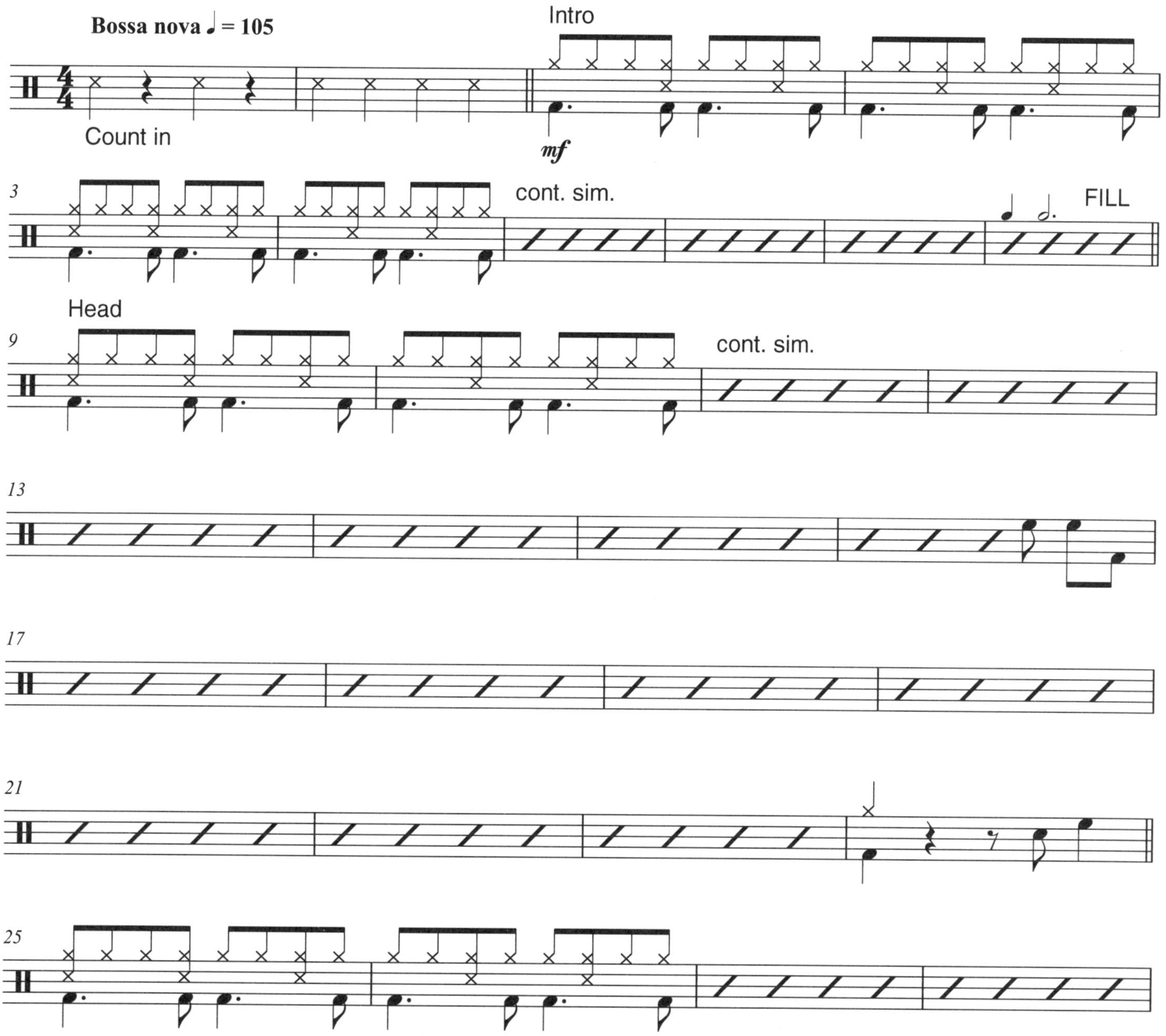

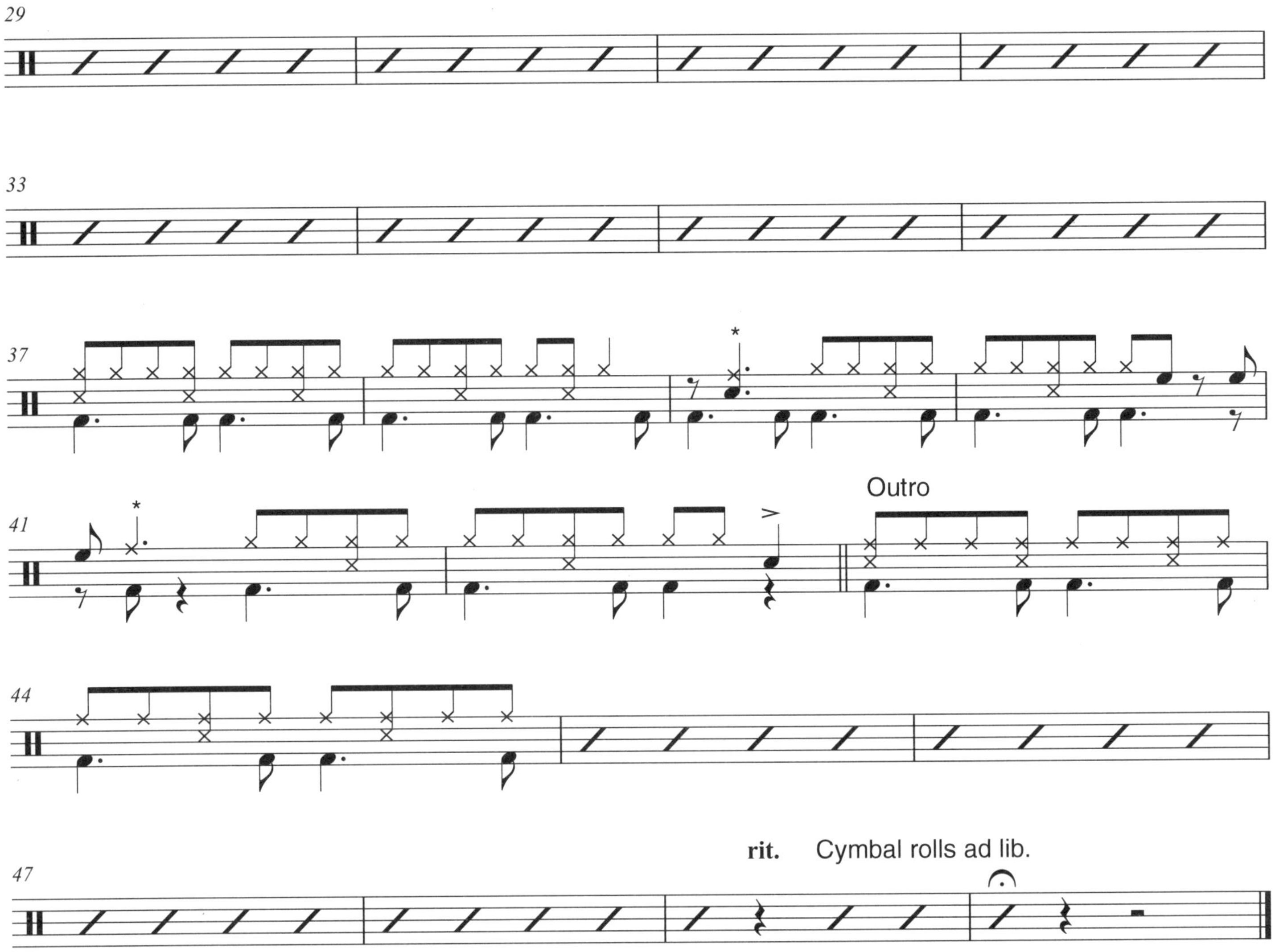

* Play either ride cymbal or light crash, as you prefer.

The shuffle

The **shuffle** is a feel with many variants. In its basic form, the first and third quaver triplet of every beat are played by the leading hand on hi hat or cymbal, creating a swinging feel.

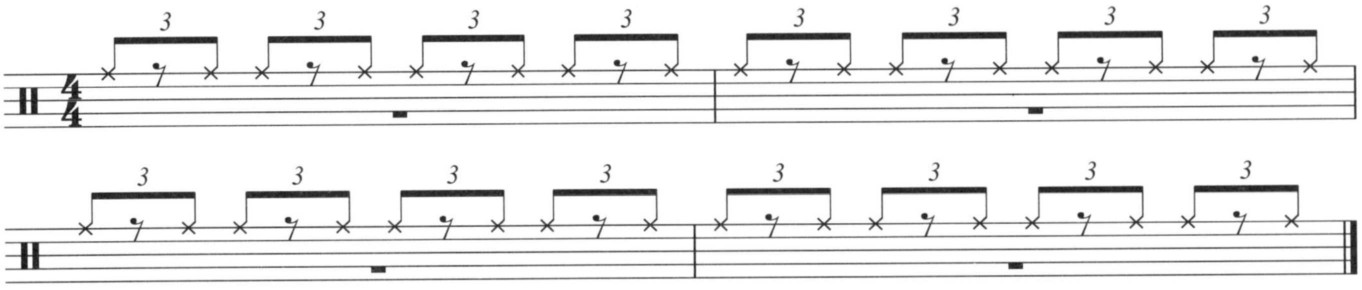

Beneath this pattern, the snare and bass drum can thicken out the groove in a variety of ways.

Three good examples of songs with shuffle grooves to listen to are as follows. 'Statesboro Blues' from The Allman Brothers *Live at Fillmore East* from 1971 features TWO drummers playing at the same time: the very disciplined Butch Trucks and Jai Johanny 'Jaimoe' Johanson. Also in a blues style is Chris Layton's playing on 'Pride and Joy' from guitarist Stevie Ray Vaughan's 1983 album *Texas Flood*. Finally, the 1967 pop hit 'Jimmy Mack' from Martha Reeves and the Vandellas features the drummer Richard 'Pistol' Allen.

Here are some examples of simple shuffle grooves.

Performance piece

Get to know how the piece should sound by listening to the demo track. Then you can start to play the piece along with the backing track.

 Tracks 12a, 12b & 12c

Shuffle the Deck

Congratulations

You've now completed these eight stages of study and should be well equipped to enjoy making more music, be that having a jam with your friends, working up a set with a band, playing in a concert band or big band at school or just playing at home.

Your understanding of music theory and notation is also thorough enough to support you in your study for Trinity Rock & Pop or Trinity College London drum kit exams at Grades 3 and 4.

Notes and rests reference chart

Examples in 4/4

Semibreve
(Whole note)
4 beats

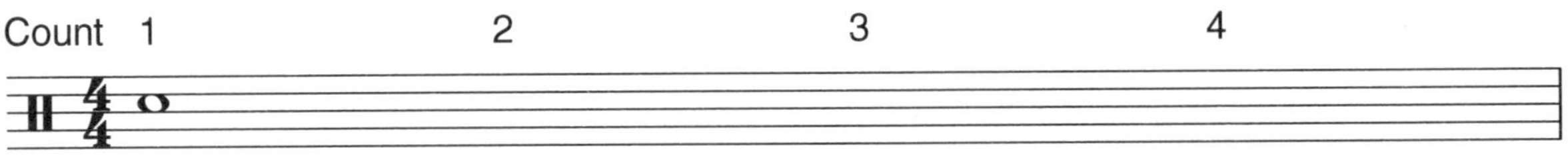

Minim
(Half note)
2 beats

Crotchet
(Quarter note)
1 beat

Quaver
(Eighth note)
½ of a beat

Triplet quaver
(Eighth-note triplet)
⅓ of a beat

Semiquaver
(16th note)
¼ of a beat

Triplet semiquaver
(16th-note triplet)
⅙ of a beat

Demisemiquaver
(32nd note)
⅛ of a beat

Examples in 12/8

Remember adding a dot to the note lengthens the note by half its original value.

Dotted crotchet
(dotted quarter note)
1½ beats

Quavers in 12/8
(Eighth notes in 12/8)

42

Rests

Semibreve rest
(Whole-note rest)
4 beats (in 4/4)

> **Note:**
> In 4/4 time, this type of rest will last for four beats. If this rest is seen in any other time signature, it will last for one complete bar.

Minim rest
(Half-note rest)
2 beats

Crotchet rest
(Quarter-note rest)
1 beat

Quaver rest
(Eighth-note rest)
½ of a beat

Semiquaver rest
(16th-note rest)
¼ of a beat

> **Did you know?**
> Dots can also be added to rests. By adding a dot to a rest it lengthens the rest by half its original value.

Recommended listening

The study of any instrument should involve as much listening as possible. There are so many fantastic players, past and present, who can entertain and inspire us.

My favourites, and top of many drummers' lists are Buddy Rich and Steve Gadd. Other great names, from a wide range of musical styles, are:

Travis Barker	Vinnie Colaiuta	Elvin Jones	Bernard Purdie
Cindy Blackman	Pete DePoe	Philly Joe Jones	Herlin Riley
Louie Bellson	Sheila E	Jim Keltner	Max Roach
Hal Blaine	Allan Ganley	Gene Krupa	Steve Smith
John Bonham	David Garibaldi	Zigaboo Modeliste	Bill Stewart
Dennis Chambers	Dave Grohl	Ian Paice	Ed Thigpen
Kenny Clare	Jeff Hamilton	Shawn Pelton	Tony Thompson
Billy Cobham	Richie Hayward	Jeff Porcaro	Dave Weckl

Recording credits

Thank you to my friends and fabulous players who played on the tracks for this book. Particular thanks to Tom Fleming, Paul Fitzgerald and my nephew Adam for their excellent work.

1. This Old Heart (Adam Double/George Double)
Vocal, Guitars and Bass Guitar: Adam Double • Backing Vocals: Joanna Eden • Drums: George Double

2. A Secret (Adam Double/George Double)
Vocal, Guitar, Keyboards and Bass Guitar: Adam Double • Drums: George Double

3. No More a Stranger (George Double)
Vocal: Joanna Eden • Guitar: Tom Fleming • Electric Piano: Chris Ingham
• Bass Guitar and Backing Vocal: Adam Double • Drums: George Double

4. A Pair of Snares (George Double)
Snare Drum: George Double

5. All about the Bounce (George Double)
Saxophone: Derek Nash • Guitar: Tom Fleming • Keyboards: Chris Ingham • Bass Guitar: Adam Double
• Drums and Percussion: George Double

6. Wayfaring Stranger (Trad. Arr. George Double)
Vocal: Joanna Eden • Trumpet: Paul Higgs • Saxophone: Derek Nash • Piano: Chris Ingham
• Bass Guitar: Adam Double • Drums: George Double

7. Indiana (Trad. Arr. George Double)
Trumpet: Paul Higgs • Saxophone: Derek Nash • Piano: Chris Ingham • Double Bass: Russell Swift
• Drums: George Double

8. I'll Be Alright (Adam Double/George Double)
Vocal, Guitar, Keyboards and Bass Guitar: Adam Double • Drums: George Double

9. All for Nothing (Adam Double/George Double)
Vocal, Guitar, Keyboards and Bass Guitar: Adam Double • Backing Vocal: Joanna Eden
• Drums: George Double

10. The Lilting Banshee (Trad. Arr. Tom Fleming/George Double)
Cello: Sophie Gledhill • Guitars, Bass and Whistles: Tom Fleming • Drums: George Double

11. Indian Summer (Victor Herbert/Al Dubin Arr. George Double)
Vocal: Joanna Eden • Saxophone: Derek Nash • Guitar: Tom Fleming • Piano: Chris Ingham
• Double Bass: Russell Swift • Drums: George Double

12. Shuffle the Deck (George Double)
Saxophone: Derek Nash • Trumpet: Paul Higgs • Guitar: Tom Fleming • Piano: Chris Ingham
• Bass Guitar: Adam Double • Drums: George Double

Recorded at various locations during the spring of 2020.
Drums recorded by Paul Fitzgerald at Saints Studios, near Bungay, Suffolk.
Produced by Tom Fleming